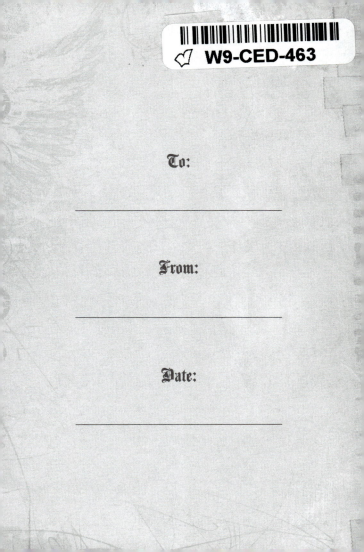

To:

_____

From:

_____

Date:

_____

© 2010 Ellie Claire™ Gift & Paper Corp.
a division of Worthy Media, Inc.
Brentwood, TN 37207
www.ellieclaire.com

For I Know the Plans I Have for You (Eagle)

A *Pocket Inspirations* Book

ISBN 978-1-60936-123-5

Scripture references are from the following sources: The Holy Bible, New
International Version® NIV®. Copyright © 1973, 1978, 1984 by Biblica,
Inc.™ Used by permission of Zondervan. All rights reserved worldwide. The
New King James Version (NKJV). Copyright © 1982 by Thomas Nelson,
Inc. Used by permission. The Holy Bible, New Living Translation® (NLT),
copyright © 1996, 2004. Used by permission of Tyndale House Publishers,
Inc., Wheaton, Illinois. *The Message* (MSG) © 1993, 1994, 1995, 1996, 2000,
2001, 2002 by Eugene Peterson. Used by permission of NavPress, Colorado
Springs, CO. The New Century Version® (NCV). Copyright © 1987, 1988,
1991 by Thomas Nelson, Inc. Used by permission. All rights reserved. The
New American Standard Bible® (NASB), Copyright © 1960, 1962, 1963,
1968, 1971, 1972, 1973, 1975, 1977, 1995 by The Lockman Foundation.
Used by permission. All rights reserved.

Excluding Scripture verses and deity pronouns, in some quotations references
to women and feminine pronouns have been replaced with gender-neutral
or masculine references. Additionally, in some quotations we have carefully
updated verb forms and wordings that may distract modern readers.

Stock or custom editions of Ellie Claire titles may be purchased in bulk for
educational, business, ministry, fundraising, or sales promotional use. For
information, please e-mail info@ellieclaire.com.

Compiled by Marilyn Jansen
Designed by Lisa and Jeff Franke

Printed in U.S.A.

For I know the plans I have for you

Jeremiah 29:11

Pi Pocket
INSPIRATIONS

Ellie Claire

...inspired by life

A Bright Future

Your future is as bright as the promises of God.

A. JUDSON

No eye has seen, no ear has heard,
and no mind has imagined what
God has prepared for those who love him.

1 CORINTHIANS 2:9 NLT

What we feel, think, and do this moment influences
both our present and the future in ways we may
never know. Begin. Start right where you are.
Consider your possibilities and find inspiration...
to add more meaning and zest to your life.

ALEXANDRA STODDARD

Commit to the LORD whatever you do,
and your plans will succeed.

PROVERBS 16:3 NIV

The future lies before you like a field of driven snow,
Be careful how you tread it, for every step will show.

You have been called to one glorious hope for the
future. There is one Lord...and one God and Father,
who is over all and in all and living through all.

EPHESIANS 4:4–6 NLT

God has designs on our future...and He has designed
us for the future. He has given us something to do in
the future that no one else can do.

RUTH SENTER

"For I know the plans I have for you,"
declares the LORD, "plans to prosper you and not to
harm you, plans to give you hope and a future."

JEREMIAH 29:11 NIV

Dreams and Goals

There is nothing like a dream to create the future.

VICTOR HUGO

Hope deferred makes the heart sick,
but a dream fulfilled is a tree of life.

PROVERB 13:12 NLT

A dream becomes a goal when action
is taken toward its achievement.

BO BENNETT

I have not achieved it, but I focus on this one thing:
Forgetting the past and looking forward to what
lies ahead, I press on to reach the end of the race
and receive the heavenly prize for which God,
through Christ Jesus, is calling us.

PHILIPPIANS 3:13–14 NLT

Shoot for the moon. Even if you miss,
you'll land among the stars.

LES BROWN

Every good action and every perfect gift
is from God. These good gifts come down
from the Creator of the sun, moon, and stars,
who does not change like their shifting shadows.

JAMES 1:17 NCV

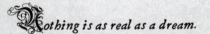othing is as real as a dream.
The world can change around you, but your dream
will not. Responsibilities need not erase it. Duties
need not obscure it. Because the dream
is within you, no one can take it away.

TOM CLANCY

There is surely a future hope for you,
and your hope will not be cut off.

PROVERBS 23:18 NIV

Go confidently in the direction of your dreams.
Live the life you have imagined.

HENRY DAVID THOREAU

Armor of God

Therefore take up the whole armor of God,
that you may be able to withstand in the evil day,
and having done all, to stand.

EPHESIANS 6:13 NKJV

Lord, protect us from temptation today.
Strengthen us so we are able to say no! Give us
persistence to turn away from trouble again
and again. Lord, help us not to be blinded by
our wants and desires or by our need to be
like everybody else. Help us to be different.
Help us to stand firm, even if we stand by
ourselves. For we are never alone—You are
always with us. Amen.

MARILYN JANSEN

Despite all these things, overwhelming victory is ours
through Christ, who loved us. And I am convinced that
nothing can ever separate us from God's love.

ROMANS 8:37–38 NLT

Where are you going?
Where is your soul?
Is it in peace?
If troubled, why?
How are you fulfilling the duties of the position?
What are they?
What effort have you made to amend your disposition,
and conquer your sins?
Have you been faithful to the light God has given you?
What means should you use, especially with regard to
your most besetting sin or temptation?
Have you fought against it?
Have you thought about it at all?

PERE RAVIGNAN

Have Compassion

Society needs people who...know how to be
compassionate and honest.... You can't run
the society on data and computers alone.

ALVIN TOFFLER

*What happens when we live God's way? He
brings gifts into our lives...things like affection
for others, exuberance about life...a sense of
compassion in the heart, and a conviction that
a basic holiness permeates things and people.*

GALATIANS 5:22–23 MSG

God comforts all His children.
He has compassion on those who are hurting.
He soothes their souls and gives them peace.

Praise be to the God and Father of our
Lord Jesus Christ, the Father of compassion and the
God of all comfort, who comforts us in all our troubles,
so that we can comfort those in any trouble with the
comfort we ourselves have received from God.

2 CORINTHIANS 1:3–4 NIV

There never was any heart truly great and generous,
that was not also tender and compassionate.

ROBERT SOUTH

Be agreeable, be sympathetic, be loving,
be compassionate, be humble. That goes for all of
you, no exceptions. No retaliation. No sharp-tongued
sarcasm. Instead, bless—that's your job, to bless.
You'll be a blessing and also get a blessing.

1 PETER 3:8–9 MSG

The compassionate person feels with God's heart.

The Road Ahead

My Lord God, I have no idea where I am going.
I do not see the road ahead of me. I cannot know for
certain where it will end.... But I believe that the desire
to please You does in fact please You. And I hope
I have that desire in all that I am doing. I hope that
I will never do anything apart from that desire.
And I know that if I do this, You will lead me by
the right road though I may know nothing about it.
Therefore will I trust You always, though I may seem
to be lost and in the shadow of death. I will not fear,
for You are ever with me. And You will never leave
me to face my perils alone.

Thomas Merton

I would rather walk with God in the dark
than go alone in the light.

Mary Gardiner Brainard

You are a chosen people, a royal priesthood,
a holy nation, a people belonging to God,
that you may declare the praises of him who called
you out of darkness into his wonderful light.

1 PETER 2:9 NIV

Heaven often seems distant and unknown,
but if He who made the road...is our guide,
we need not fear to lose the way.

HENRY VAN DYKE

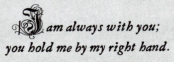
*I am always with you;
you hold me by my right hand.*

PSALM 73:23 NIV

Stay Focused

Goals provide the energy source that powers our lives.
One of the best ways we can get the most from
the energy we have is to focus it. That is what goals
can do for us; concentrate our energy.

DENIS WAITLEY

Many an opportunity is lost because one
is out looking for four-leaf clovers.

Let us not grow weary while doing good,
for in due season we shall reap if we do not lose heart.
Therefore, as we have opportunity, let us do good to all.

GALATIANS 6:9–10 NKJV

*Look straight ahead, and fix your eyes on what
lies before you. Mark out a straight path for your
feet; stay on the safe path. Don't get sidetracked;
keep your feet from following evil.*

PROVERBS 4:25–27 NLT

All who have accomplished great things have had
a great aim, have fixed their gaze on a goal which was high,
one which sometimes seemed impossible.

ORISON SWETT MARDEN

I'm not saying that I have this all together, that I have it
made. But I am well on my way, reaching out for Christ,
who has so wondrously reached out for me.

PHILIPPIANS 3:12 MSG

We need a focus. A main thing. Something bigger
than skin cream or tennis shoes that reminds us
of the purpose of it all. If we expect to regain
a more simple heart, a more centered pace for our day,
we need to order our lives in specific ways.

DAVID AND BARBARA SORENSEN

Be Strong

Your God has commanded your strength;
Strengthen, O God, what You have done for us.

PSALM 68:28 NKJV

Each battle teaches you to fight,
Each foe to be a braver knight,
Armed with His might.

J. H. BOHMER

Do not be afraid, nor be dismayed;
be strong and of good courage.

JOSHUA 10:25 NKJV

I place no hope in my strength, nor in my works:
but all my confidence is in God my protector,
who never abandons those who have put
all their hope and thought in Him.

FRANÇOIS RABELAIS

The strongest people aren't always the people who win,
but the people who don't give up when they lose.

ASHLEY HODGESON

Never talk defeat. Use words like hope,
belief, faith, victory.

NORMAN VINCENT PEALE

*Be strong and of good courage, do not fear nor
be afraid of them; for the LORD your God,
He is the One who goes with you.
He will not leave you nor forsake you.*

DEUTERONOMY 31:6 NKJV

Do not pray for easy lives; pray to be stronger....
Do not pray for tasks equal to your powers; pray for
powers equal to your tasks. Then the doing of your
work shall be not miracle, but you shall be a miracle.
Every day you shall wonder at yourself, at the riches of
life which have come to you by the grace of God.

PHILLIPS BROOKS

Keep Knocking

Perseverance is a great element of success.
If you only knock long enough and loud enough
at the gate, you are sure to wake up somebody.

HENRY WADSWORTH LONGFELLOW

Ask and it will be given to you;
seek and you will find; knock and the door
will be opened to you. For everyone
who asks receives; he who seeks finds;
and to him who knocks, the door will be opened.

MATTHEW 7:7–8 NIV

Most of the important things in the world have
been accomplished by people who have kept
on trying when there seemed to be no hope at all.

DALE CARNEGIE

We also rejoice in our sufferings, because we
know that suffering produces perseverance;
perseverance, character; and character, hope.
And hope does not disappoint us, because
God has poured out His love into our hearts.

ROMANS 5:3–5 NIV

Hope means hoping when things are hopeless,
or it is no virtue at all.... As long as matters
are really hopeful, hope is mere flattery
or platitude; it is only when everything
is hopeless that hope begins to be a strength.

G. K. CHESTERTON

As you know, we consider blessed those who have
persevered. You have heard of Job's perseverance
and have seen what the Lord finally brought about.
The Lord is full of compassion and mercy.

JAMES 5:11 NIV

A Work of Art

Each one of us is God's special work of art.
Through us, He teaches and inspires, delights
and encourages, informs and uplifts all those who
view our lives. God, the master artist, is most
concerned about expressing Himself——His thoughts
and His intentions——through what He paints
in our character.... [He] wants to paint a beautiful
portrait of His Son in and through your life.
A painting like no other in all of time.

JONI EARECKSON TADA

*I will give thanks to You, for I am fearfully
and wonderfully made; wonderful are Your
works, and my soul knows it very well.*

PSALM 139:14 NASB

Whether we are poets or parents or teachers
or artists or gardeners, we must start where we are
and use what we have. In the process of creation
and relationship, what seems mundane and trivial may
show itself to be holy, precious, part of a pattern.

LUCI SHAW

Hold on to the pattern of wholesome teaching
you learned from me—a pattern shaped by the faith
and love that you have in Christ Jesus.

2 TIMOTHY 1:13 NLT

When we gaze at nature, at a loved one,
at a work of art, our soul immediately recognizes
and is drawn to the face of God.

MARGARET BROWNLEY

The Road

You have brains in your head.
You have feet in your shoes.
You can steer yourself in any direction you choose.
You're on your own. And you know what you know.
You are the [one] who'll decide where to go.

DR. SEUSS

If the LORD delights in a man's way, he makes
his steps firm; though he stumble, he will not fall,
for the LORD upholds him with his hand.

PSALM 37:23–24 NIV

God, who has led you safely on so far,
will lead you on to the end. Be altogether
at rest in the loving holy confidence which you
ought to have in His heavenly providence.

FRANCIS DE SALES

From now on every road you travel
Will take you to GOD.
Follow the Covenant signs;
Read the charted directions.

We may not all reach God's ideal for us, but with His
help we may move in that direction day by day as we
relate every detail of our lives to Him.

*In all your ways acknowledge Him,
And He shall direct your paths.*

Today Is Unique

Every day we live is a priceless gift of God,
loaded with possibilities to learn something new,
to gain fresh insights.

DALE EVANS ROGERS

This is the day the LORD has made;
we will rejoice and be glad in it.

PSALM 118:24 NKJV

Today is unique! It has never occurred before and it
will never be repeated. At midnight it will end, quietly,
suddenly, totally. Forever. But the hours between now
and then are opportunities with eternal possibilities.

CHARLES R. SWINDOLL

Go after a life of love as if your life depended on
it—because it does. Give yourselves to the gifts God
gives you. Most of all, try to proclaim his truth.

1 CORINTHIANS 14:1 MSG

Time is a very precious gift of God; so precious
that it's only given to us moment by moment.

AMELIA BARR

I will bless the LORD at all times:
His praise shall continually be in my mouth.

PSALM 34:1 NKJV

Each day offers time to draw closer to God
and take new steps toward living with purpose.

*Be careful how you live.... Make the most of
every opportunity.... Don't act thoughtlessly,
but understand what the Lord wants you to do.*

EPHESIANS 5:15–17 NLT

One Plus God

Do not be afraid or discouraged, for the LORD
will personally go ahead of you. He will be with you;
he will neither fail you nor abandon you.

DEUTERONOMY 31:8 NLT

God does not require from you to be sinless
when you come before Him, but He does require
you to be unceasing in your perseverance.
He does not require that you shall never have fallen;
but he does require unwearied efforts. He does not
require you to win, but He does require you to fight.

FREDERICK TEMPLE

With God all things are possible.

MATTHEW 19:26 KJV

*When all else is gone,
God is left and nothing changes Him.*

HANNAH WHITALL SMITH

Be strong and very courageous.

JOSHUA 1:7 NASB

One song can spark a moment
One flower can wake the dream
One tree can start a forest
One bird can herald spring
One smile begins a friendship
One handclasp lifts a soul
One start can guide a ship at sea
One word can frame the goal
One vote can change a nation
One sunbeam lights a room
One candle wipes our darkness
One laugh will conquer gloom
One step must start each journey
One word must start a prayer
One hope will raise our spirits
One touch can show you care
One voice can speak with wisdom
One heart can know what's true
One life can make a difference
That difference starts with you.

Funny Bones

It is pleasing to God whenever you rejoice
or laugh from the bottom of your heart.

MARTIN LUTHER

Laugh with your happy friends when they're happy.

ROMANS 12:15 MSG

The leadership instinct you are born with
is the backbone. You develop the funny bone
and the wishbone that go with it.

ELAINE AGATHER

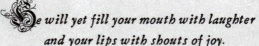*e will yet fill your mouth with laughter
and your lips with shouts of joy.*

JOB 8:21 NIV

Stick through the hard times,
one day you will laugh at them.

SHERRI M.

And now, GOD, do it again—
bring rains to our drought-stricken lives....
So those who went off with heavy hearts
will come home laughing, with armloads of blessing.

PSALM 126:4–6 MSG

If you want to be truly happy, you won't find
it on an endless quest for more stuff.
You'll find it in receiving God's generosity
and then passing that generosity along.

BILL HYBELS

Praise the LORD.
Blessed is the man who fears the LORD,
who finds great delight in his commands.

PSALM 112:1 NIV

Seeds of Value

Don't judge each day by the harvest you reap
but by the seeds that you plant.

ROBERT LOUIS STEVENSON

Plant your seed in the morning and keep busy
all afternoon, for you don't know if profit will come
from one activity or another—or maybe both.

ECCLESIASTES 11:6 NLT

The true meaning of life is to plant trees,
under whose shade you do not expect to sit.

NELSON HENDERSON

*It's not important who does the planting,
or who does the watering. What's important is that
God makes the seed grow. The one who plants
and the one who waters work together with the
same purpose. And both will be rewarded.*

1 CORINTHIANS 3:7–8 NLT

I will consider my earthly existence to have been
wasted unless I can recall a loving family, a consistent
investment in the lives of people, and an earnest
attempt to serve the God who made me.

James Dobson

When you're kind to others, you help yourself;
when you're cruel to others, you hurt yourself.

Proverbs 11:17 msg

We must begin to make the kind of investment
of personal time and commitment which will assure
that those who come after us will live as well.

Charles W. Bray III

Press On

Oh, that we might know the LORD! Let us press on to know him. He will respond to us as surely as the arrival of dawn or the coming of rains in early spring.

HOSEA 6:3 NLT

There are four steps to accomplishment:
Plan Purposefully.
Prepare Prayerfully.
Proceed Positively.
Pursue Persistently.

Nothing in the world can take the place of persistence. Talent will not; nothing is more common than unsuccessful men with talent. Genius will not; unrewarded genius is almost a proverb. Education will not; the world is full of educated derelicts. Persistence and determination are omnipotent. The slogan "press on" has solved and always will solve the problems of the human race. No person was ever honored for what he received. Honor has been the reward for what he gave.

CALVIN COOLIDGE

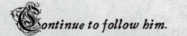

Continue to follow him.
Let your roots grow down into him,
and let your lives be built on him.
Then your faith will grow strong
in the truth you were taught.

COLOSSIANS 2:6–7 NLT

Listen to the mustn'ts, child,
Listen to the don'ts—
Listen to the shouldn'ts, the impossibles, the won'ts—
Listen to the never haves,
Then listen close to me.
Anything can happen, child.
Anything can be.

SHEL SILVERSTEIN

Bright Dreams

No matter what your age or your situation,
your dreams are achievable. Whether you're five or 105,
you have a lifetime ahead of you!

Oh, how sweet the light of day,
and how wonderful to live in the sunshine!
Even if you live a long time, don't take a single day
for granted. Take delight in each light-filled hour.

ECCLESIASTES 11:7–8 MSG

A #2 pencil and a dream can take you anywhere.

JOYCE MEYER

Toss your faded dreams not into a trash bin
but into a drawer where you are likely
to rummage some bright morning.

ROBERT BRAULT

*The important thing really is not the deed
well done or the medal that you possess, but the
dedication and dreams out of which they grow.*

ROBERT H. BENSON

Steep your life in God-reality, God-initiative,
God-provisions. Don't worry about missing out.
You'll find all your everyday human concerns will be met.

MATTHEW 6:33 MSG

The victory of success is half won when one gains
the habit of setting goals and achieving them.
Even the most tedious chore will become endurable
as you parade through each day convinced that
every task, no matter how menial or boring, brings
you closer to fulfilling your dreams.

OG MANDINO

Value

You are valuable just because you exist.
Not because of what you do or what you have done,
but simply because you are. Just think about
the way Jesus honors you...and smile.

MAX LUCADO

Life is but a brief moment between eternities.
There is no better time than now to assess the values
which are worthy of our existence on this earth.

JAMES DOBSON

God not only knows us, but He values us highly
in spite of all He knows. "You are worth more than
many sparrows."... You and I are the creatures He prizes
above the rest of His creation. We are made in His
image and He sacrificed His Son that each one of us
might be one with Him. Sparrows are sold at two for
a penny; we were bought with a much higher price.

JOHN FISHER

Are not five sparrows sold for two copper coins?
And not one of them is forgotten before God.
But the very hairs of your head are
all numbered. Do not fear therefore;
you are of more value than many sparrows.

LUKE 12:6–7 NKJV

*We are of such value to God that He
came to live among us...and to guide us
home. He will go to any length to seek us,
even to being lifted high upon the cross
to draw us back to Himself. We can only
respond by loving God for His love.*

CATHERINE OF SIENA

Learn It All

Get over the idea that only children should spend their
time in study. Be a student so long as you still have
something to learn, and this will mean all your life.

HENRY L. DOHERTY

I'm asking God for one thing, only one thing:
To live with Him in His house my whole life long.
I'll contemplate His beauty; I'll study at His feet.

PSALM 27:4 MSG

It's what you learn after you know it all that counts.

HARRY S. TRUMAN

A wise man will hear and increase learning, and
a man of understanding will attain wise counsel.

PROVERBS 1:5 NKJV

A study of the nature and character of God is the most
practical project anyone can engage in. Knowing about
God is crucially important for the living of our lives.

J. I. PACKER

Continue in what you have learned and have become
convinced of, because you know those from whom
you learned it, and how from infancy you have known
the holy Scriptures, which are able to make you wise
for salvation through faith in Christ Jesus.

2 TIMOTHY 3:14–15 NIV

A single conversation across the table with
a wise man is worth a month's study of books.

CHINESE PROVERB

Working Together

I feel simply carried along each hour, doing my part
in a plan which is far beyond myself. This sense
of cooperation with God in little things is what
so astonishes me, for I never have felt this
way before. I need something, and turn round
to find it waiting for me. I must work, to be sure,
but there is God working along with me.

FRANK LAUBACH

*The price of success is hard work, dedication
to the job at hand, and the determination
that whether we win or lose, we have applied
the best of ourselves to the task at hand.*

VINCENT T. LOMBARDI

It helps, now and then, to step back and take a long view. The kingdom [of God] is not only beyond our efforts, it is even beyond our vision. We accomplish in our lifetime only a tiny fraction of the magnificent enterprise that is God's work. Nothing we do is complete, which is a way of saying that the kingdom always lies beyond us.... We cannot do everything, and there is a sense of liberation in realizing that. This enables us to do something, and to do it very well. It may be incomplete, but it is a beginning, a step along the way, an opportunity for the Lord's grace to enter and do the rest. We may never see the end results, but that is the difference between the master builder and the worker.

OSCAR ROMERO

Step of Faith

Don't be afraid to take a big step if one is indicated;
you can't cross a chasm in two small jumps.

DAVID LLOYD GEORGE

You took a risk trusting Me, and now you're
healed and whole. Live well, live blessed!

LUKE 8:48 MSG

When you come to the end of all the light
you know, and it's time to step into the darkness
of the unknown, faith is knowing that one of two
things shall happen: Either you will be given something
solid to stand on or you will be taught to fly.

EDWARD TELLER

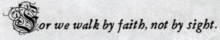 *For we walk by faith, not by sight.*

2 CORINTHIANS 5:7 NKJV

Optimism is the faith that leads to achievement.
Nothing can be done without hope and confidence.

HELEN KELLER

Be strong and let your heart take courage,
All you who hope in the LORD.

PSALM 31:24 NASB

From the little spark may burst a mighty flame.

DANTE

May he give you the power to accomplish all
the good things your faith prompts you to do.

2 THESSALONIANS 1:11 NLT

Make the Best

May He grant you according to your heart's desire,
And fulfill all your purpose.

PSALM 20:4 NKJV

Common sense is the measure of the possible;
it is composed of experience and prevision;
it is calculation applied to life.

HENRI FRÉDÉRIC AMIEL

For the LORD grants wisdom! From his mouth
come knowledge and understanding. He grants
a treasure of common sense to the honest.
He is a shield to those who walk with integrity.

PROVERBS 2:6–7 NLT

I will praise you forever for what you have done;
in your name I will hope, for your name is good.
I will praise you in the presence of your saints.

PSALM 52:9 NIV

Things turn out best for the people who make
the best out of the way things turn out.

ART LINKLETTER

We know that God causes everything to work
together for the good of those who love God
and are called according to his purpose for them.

ROMANS 8:28 NLT

Invincible

Hope of final victory is ours, if we only remember that we are fighting God's battles. And can He know defeat? He who is the God of the great world around us is the God of the little world within. It is He who is fighting in you; you are but His soldier, guided by His wisdom, strengthened by His might, shielded by His love. Keep your will united to the will of God, and the final defeat is impossible; for He is invincible.

GEORGE BODY

Courage, it shall be well: we follow a conquering general; yes, who has conquered already; and He that has conquered for us shall ever conquer in us.

ROBERT LEIGHTON

Behold, God himself is with us.

2 CHRONICLES 13:12 KJV

Oh, for trust that brings the triumph
When defeat seems strangely near!
Oh, for faith that changes fighting
Into victory's ringing cheer—
Faith triumphant, knowing not defeat or fear!

HERBERT BOOTH

You must not fear them,
for the LORD your God Himself fights for you.

DEUTERONOMY 3:22 NKJV

When real faith grips you, you develop a mind-set
that looks for the best in everything, refuses
to give up, finds a way around (or through)
every obstacle, and presses on to victory.

NORMAN VINCENT PEALE

Freely Share

You can't live a perfect day without doing something
for someone who will never be able to repay you.

JOHN WOODEN

Each of you has received a gift to use to serve others.
Be good servants of God's various gifts of grace.

1 PETER 4:10 NCV

Giving is a joy if we do it in the right spirit.
It all depends on whether we think of it as
"What can I spare?" or as "What can I share?"

ESTHER YORK BURKHOLDER

Those who will use their skill and constructive
imagination to see how much they can give
for a dollar, instead of how little they can
give for a dollar, are bound to succeed.

HENRY FORD

This service you do not only helps the needs of God's people, it also brings many more thanks to God. It is a proof of your faith. Many people will praise God because you obey the Good News...and because you freely share with them and with all others.

2 CORINTHIANS 9:12–13 NCV

The secret of life is that all we have
and are is a gift of grace to be shared.

LLOYD JOHN OGILVIE

Remind the people...to be ready to do whatever
is good...to be peaceable and considerate, and to
show true humility toward all men.

TITUS 3:1–2 NIV

Learn More

Pay close attention, friend, to what your
father tells you; never forget what
you learned at your mother's knee.

PROVERBS 1:8 MSG

The purpose of learning is growth,
and our minds, unlike our bodies,
can continue growing as we continue to live.

MORTIMER ADLER

*The mind of a person with understanding gets
knowledge; the wise person listens to learn more.*

PROVERBS 18:15 NCV

You learn something every day if you pay attention.

RAY LEBLOND

Teach the wise, and they will become even wiser;
teach good people, and they will learn even more.

PROVERBS 9:9 NCV

No matter how some may think themselves
accomplished, when they set out to learn
a new language, science, or the bicycle,
they have entered a new realm as truly as if they
were a child newly born into the world.

FRANCES WILLARD

Don't copy the behavior and customs of this
world, but let God transform you into a new
person by changing the way you think.
Then you will learn to know God's will for you,
which is good and pleasing and perfect.

ROMANS 12:2 NLT

Rewarding Work

There's no thrill in easy sailing
when the skies are clear and blue,
There's no joy in merely doing things
which anyone can do.
But there is some satisfaction
that is mighty sweet to take,
When you reach a destination
that you thought you'd never make.

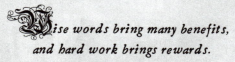

*Wise words bring many benefits,
and hard work brings rewards.*

PROVERBS 12:14 NLT

Whenever it is possible, choose some
occupation which you should do
even if you did not need the money.

WILLIAM LYON PHELPS

Work with a smile on your face, always keeping
in mind that no matter who happens to be giving
the orders, you're really serving God.

EPHESIANS 6:7 MSG

The difference between something good
and something great is attention to detail.

CHARLES SWINDOLL

My heart rejoiced in all my labor;
And this was my reward from all my labor.

ECCLESIASTES 2:10 NKJV

The secret of joy in work is contained
in one word—excellence. To know how
to do something well is to enjoy it.

PEARL S. BUCK

Therefore, my beloved brethren, be steadfast,
immovable, always abounding in the work of the Lord,
knowing that your labor is not in vain in the Lord.

1 CORINTHIANS 15:58 NKJV

Dare to Dream

Your righteousness, O God,
reaches to the highest heavens.
You have done such wonderful things.
Who can compare with you, O God?

PSALM 71:19 NLT

*You can't experience success
beyond your wildest dreams until you
dare to dream something wild!*

SCOTT SORRELL

Somehow I can't believe that there are any
heights that can't be scaled by a man who knows
the secrets of making dreams come true. This special
secret...can be summarized in four Cs. They are
curiosity, confidence, courage, and constancy.

WALT DISNEY

God can do anything, you know—
far more than you could ever imagine
or guess or request in your wildest dreams!

EPHESIANS 3:20 MSG

My child, eat honey, for it is good, and the honeycomb
is sweet to the taste. In the same way, wisdom is sweet
to your soul. If you find it, you will have a bright
future, and your hopes will not be cut short.

PROVERBS 24:13–14 NLT

One hundred years from today your present income
will be inconsequential. One hundred years from
now it won't matter if you got that big break, took the
trip to Europe, or finally traded up to a Mercedes....
It will matter that you knew God.

DAVID SHIBLEY

Dear friend, listen well to my words.... Those who
discover these words live, really live; body and soul....
Keep vigilant watch over your heart;
that's where life starts.

PROVERBS 4:20–23 MSG

The Good Fight

However matters go, it is our happiness to win new
ground daily in Christ's love, and to purchase a new
piece of it daily, and to add conquest to conquest.

SAMUEL RUTHERFORD

Fight the good fight
With all your might;
Christ is your Strength, and Christ your Right;
Lay hold of life,
And it shall be
Your joy and crown eternally.

J. S. B. MONSELL

*I have fought the good fight, I have finished the
race, and I have remained faithful. And now the
prize awaits me—the crown of righteousness.*

2 TIMOTHY 4:7–8 NLT

Let the first act when waking be to place yourself,
your heart, mind, faculties, your whole being,
in God's hands. Ask Him to take entire possession
of you, to be the guide of your soul, your life, your
wisdom, your strength. He wants us to seek Him
in all our needs, that we may both know Him
truly, and draw closer and closer to Him;
and in prayer we gain an invisible force which
will triumph over seemingly hopeless difficulties.

H. L. SIDNEY LEAR

But thanks be to God, who always leads us in
triumphal procession in Christ and through
us spreads everywhere the fragrance of the
knowledge of him.

2 CORINTHIANS 2:14 NIV

It is the eternal struggle between these two
principles—right and wrong—throughout the
world. They are the two principles that have
stood face to face from the beginning of time.

ABRAHAM LINCOLN

Becoming Yourself

You must begin to think of yourself
as becoming the person you want to be.

DAVID VISCOTT

Be wise in the way you act...make the most of
every opportunity. Let your conversation be
always full of grace, seasoned with salt, so that
you may know how to answer everyone.

COLOSSIANS 4:5–6 NIV

The golden opportunity you are seeking
is in yourself. It is not in your environment;
it is not in luck or chance, or the help of others;
it is in yourself alone.

ORISON SWETT MARDEN

The most important person
to be honest with is yourself.

So, friends, confirm God's invitation to you, his choice of you. Don't put it off; do it now. Do this, and you'll have your life on a firm footing.

2 PETER 1:10–11 MSG

Becoming a leader is synonymous with becoming yourself. It is precisely that simple, and it is also that difficult.

WARREN G. BENNIS

Anyone who belongs to Christ has become a new person. The old life is gone; a new life has begun! And all of this is a gift from God.

2 CORINTHIANS 5:17–18 NLT

Destiny

Recognizing who we are in Christ and aligning
our life with God's purpose for us gives a sense
of destiny.... It gives form and direction to our life.

JEAN FLEMING

You guide me with your counsel,
leading me to a glorious destiny.

PSALM 73:24 NLT

When we live life centered around what others like,
feel, and say, we lose touch with our own identity.
I am an eternal being, created by God. I am an
individual with purpose. It's not what I get from life,
but who I am, that makes the difference.

NEVA COYLE

Live out your God-created identity. Live generously and
graciously toward others, the way God lives toward you.

MATTHEW 5:48 MSG

God has a purpose for your life,
and no one else can take your place.

I believe that nothing that happens to me is
meaningless, and that it is good for us all that it
should be so.... As I see it, I'm here for some purpose.

DIETRICH BONHOEFFER

Everything has already been decided.
It was known long ago what each person
would be. So there's no use arguing with
God about your destiny.

ECCLESIASTES 6:10 NLT

When the world around us staggers from lack of
direction, God offers purpose, hope, and certainty.

GLORIA GAITHER

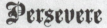Persevere

The difference between perseverance
and obstinacy is that one often comes from
a strong will, and the other from a strong won't.

HENRY WARD BEECHER

Blessed is the man who perseveres under trial,
because when he has stood the test,
he will receive the crown of life that God
has promised to those who love him.

JAMES 1:12 NIV

Life is not easy for any of us. But what of that?
We must have perseverance and above all
confidence in ourselves. We must believe
that we are gifted for something and that
this thing must be attained.

MARIE CURIE

We are made to persist.
That's how we find out who we are.

TOBIAS WOLFF

And so I tell you, keep on asking, and you will receive
what you ask for. Keep on seeking, and you will find.
Keep on knocking, and the door will be opened to you.

LUKE 11:9 NLT

Never, Never, Never Quit.

WINSTON CHURCHILL

*Let us throw off everything that hinders
and the sin that so easily entangles,
and let us run with perseverance the race
marked out for us. Let us fix our eyes on Jesus,
the author and perfecter of our faith.*

HEBREWS 12:1–2 NIV

Get Up and Lead

Leadership is a combination of strategy and character.
If you must be without one, be without the strategy.

H. NORMAN SCHWARZKOPF

Love and truth form a good leader;
sound leadership is founded on loving integrity.

PROVERBS 20:28 MSG

In simplest terms, leaders are those who know
where they want to go, and get up, and go.

JOHN ERSKINE

Without wise leadership, a nation falls;
there is safety in having many advisers.

PROVERBS 11:14 NLT

When you grow up in an environment where...
commitment and dedication is not just talked about
but lived so fully, so honestly, there is no way
that it does not take root in your being.

YOLANDA KING

Good leaders cultivate honest speech;
they love advisors who tell them the truth.

*Men make history, and not the other way
around. In periods where there is no leadership,
society stands still. Progress occurs when
courageous, skillful leaders seize the opportunity
to change things for the better.*

HARRY S. TRUMAN

Those who are wise will shine like the brightness
of the heavens, and those who lead many
to righteousness, like the stars for ever and ever.

Real leaders are ordinary people
with extraordinary determination.

Give Freely

Give, and it will be given to you. A good measure,
pressed down, shaken together and running over,
will be poured into your lap. For with the measure
you use, it will be measured to you.

LUKE 6:38 NIV

Wise are those who learn that the bottom line
doesn't always have to be their top priority.

WILLIAM A. WARD

A good name is to be chosen rather than great riches,
Loving favor rather than silver and gold.

PROVERBS 22:1 NKJV

The measure of a life, after all,
is not its duration but its donation.

CORRIE TEN BOOM

Give freely and spontaneously. Don't have a stingy heart. The way you handle matters like this triggers GOD, your God's, blessing in everything you do, all your work and ventures. There are always going to be poor and needy people among you. So I command you: Always be generous, open purse and hands, give to your neighbors in trouble, your poor and hurting neighbors.

DEUTERONOMY 15:10–11 MSG

Remember, giving is a privilege—not a duty.
Not everyone has enough to give to others.

In everything I did, I showed you that by this kind of hard work we must help the weak, remembering the words the Lord Jesus himself said: "It is more blessed to give than to receive."

ACTS 20:35 NIV

Your Success

There is a latent desire in every human being
to do something of worth that will have lasting
significance. There is a longing in most people to do
something that will make life better for others.

TONY CAMPOLO

God speaks to the crowd, but His call comes to
individuals, and through their personal obedience
He acts. He does not promise them nothing but
success, or even final victory in this life.... God does
not promise that He will protect them from trials,
from material cares, from sickness, from physical or
moral suffering. He promises only that He will be
with them in all these trials, and that He will sustain
them if they remain faithful to Him.

My life is an example to many,
because you have been my strength and protection.
That is why I can never stop praising you;
I declare your glory all day long.

PSALM 71:7–8 NLT

Give us, O Lord, a steadfast heart, which no
unworthy affection may drag downwards; give us an
unconquerable heart, which no tribulation can wear out;
give us an upright heart, which no unworthy purpose
may tempt aside. Bestow upon us also, O Lord our God,
understanding to know You, diligence to see You,
wisdom to find You, and a faithfulness that may finally
embrace You; through Jesus Christ our Lord. Amen.

THOMAS AQUINAS

Now, my son, may the LORD be with you and give
you success as you follow his directions.

1 CHRONICLES 22:11 NLT

Busyness

Don't ever let yourself get so busy that you miss
those little but important extras in life....
For it is often life's smallest pleasures...that make
the biggest and most lasting difference.

We are merely moving shadows,
and all our busy rushing ends in nothing.
We heap up wealth,
not knowing who will spend it.
And so, Lord, where do I put my hope?
My only hope is in you.

PSALM 39:6–7 NLT

There are no shortcuts to any place worth going.

BEVERLY SILLS

For what profit is it to a man if he gains
the whole world, and loses his own soul?

MATTHEW 16:26 NKJV

The busyness of life has so many of us trying desperately to fit too many activities into each day. Experts would tell us that when we are under stress, we should especially then make time to exercise. It's all the more true, for our spiritual and emotional health, that the last thing we should eliminate from our schedules is quiet time with the Lord.

You will experience God's peace, which exceeds anything we can understand. His peace will guard your hearts and minds as you live in Christ Jesus.

PHILIPPIANS 4:7 NLT

O Lord, You know how busy I must be today. If I forget You, do not You forget me.

ANTHONY ASHLEY COOPER

Learn Now

Do you know the difference between education and
experience? Education is when you read the fine print;
experience is what you get when you don't.

PETE SEEGER

Those who refuse correction hate themselves,
but those who accept correction gain understanding.
Respect for the Lord will teach you wisdom.

PROVERBS 15:32–33 NCV

Learn as much as you can while you are young,
since life becomes too busy later.

DANA STEWART SCOTT

Do not let anyone treat you as if you are
unimportant because you are young. Instead,
be an example...with your words, your actions,
your love, your faith, and your pure life.

1 TIMOTHY 4:12 NCV

Anyone who stops learning is old,
whether at twenty or eighty.

HENRY FORD

Cease listening to instruction...and you will stray
from the words of knowledge.

PROVERBS 19:27 NKJV

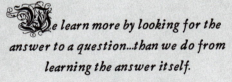

We learn more by looking for the
answer to a question...than we do from
learning the answer itself.

LLOYD ALEXANDER

You will search again for the LORD your God.
And if you search for him with all your heart
and soul, you will find him.

DEUTERONOMY 4:29 NLT

Just a Job

Regard the job you have as important but not all-important. It should honor Christ and serve others. But keep in mind the limitations to work. No job can provide...ultimate fulfillment. But if you find a sense of contentment in your work, rejoice! It is a gift from God.

DOUG SHERMAN AND WILLIAM HENDRICKS

Whenever you are asked if you can do a job, tell 'em, "Certainly I can!" Then get busy and find out how to do it.

THEODORE ROOSEVELT

May the Lord our God show us his approval and make our efforts successful.

PSALM 90:17 NLT

You learn that, whatever you are doing in life,
obstacles don't matter very much. Pain or other
circumstances can be there, but if you want to do
a job bad enough, you'll find a way to get it done.

JACK YOUNGBLOOD

The LORD your God will bless you in all your
work and in everything you put your hand to.

DEUTERONOMY 15:10 NIV

I studied the lives of great men and famous
women, and I found that the men and women
who got to the top were those who did the jobs
they had in hand with everything they had
of energy and enthusiasm and hard work.

HARRY S. TRUMAN

Never be lazy, but work hard
and serve the Lord enthusiastically.

ROMANS 12:11 NLT

On Your Heart

Let love and faithfulness never leave you; bind
them around your neck, write them on the tablet
of your heart. Then you will win favor and a good
name in the sight of God and man. Trust in the
LORD with all your heart and lean not on your own
understanding; in all your ways acknowledge him,
and he will make your paths straight.

PROVERBS 3:3–6 NIV

The road to the head lies through the heart.

AMERICAN PROVERB

Learn to love appropriately.
You need to use your head and test your feelings
so that your love is sincere and intelligent.

PHILIPPIANS 1:9–10 MSG

Those who are steadily learning how to love
are enabled to do this because the very love of God,
Himself, has been put into our hearts.

EUGENIA PRICE

I will give them singleness of heart and put a new spirit
within them. I will take away their stony, stubborn
heart and give them a tender, responsive heart.

EZEKIEL 11:19 NLT

The riches that are in the heart cannot be stolen.

RUSSIAN PROVERB

I want them to be strengthened and joined
together with love so that they may be rich in
their understanding. This leads to their knowing
fully God's secret, that is, Christ himself.

COLOSSIANS 2:2 NCV

The head learns new things, but the heart
forevermore practices old experiences.

HENRY WARD BEECHER

Stick Together

Friends are an indispensable part of a meaningful life.
They are the ones who share our burdens and multiply
our blessings. A true friend sticks by us in our joys
and sorrows. In good times and bad, we need friends
who will pray for us, listen to us, and lend a comforting
hand and an understanding ear when needed.

BEVERLY LaHAYE

Bring bread to the table and your friends
will bring their joy to share.

FRENCH PROVERB

There are "friends" who destroy each other,
but a real friend sticks closer than a brother.

PROVERBS 18:24 NLT

A friend is somebody who loves us
with understanding, as well as emotion.

ROBERT LOUIS STEVENSON

An open rebuke
is better than hidden love!
Wounds from a sincere friend
are better than many kisses from an enemy.

PROVERBS 27:5–6 NLT

Hold a true friend with both your hands.

NIGERIAN PROVERB

One of life's greatest treasures is the love
that binds hearts together in friendship.

Two people are better off than one,
for they can help each other succeed. If one person
falls, the other can reach out and help.

ECCLESIASTES 4:9–10 NLT

Friendship is the only cement that
will ever hold the world together.

WOODROW WILSON

Well Done

There is much satisfaction in work well done,
but there can be no happiness equal to the joy
of finding a heart that understands.

VICTOR ROBINSOLL

The gossip of bad people gets them in trouble;
the conversation of good people keeps them out of it.
Well-spoken words bring satisfaction;
well-done work has its own reward.

PROVERBS 12:13–14 MSG

I would give more for the private esteem and love
of one than for the public praise of ten thousand.

W. E. ALGER

Good friend, don't forget all I've taught you;
take to heart my commands. They'll help you live
a long, long time, a long life lived full and well.

PROVERBS 3:1–2 MSG

Let us begin from this moment to acknowledge
Him in all our ways, and do everything,
whatsoever we do, as service to Him
and for His glory, depending upon Him alone
for wisdom, and strength...and patience.

HANNAH WHITALL SMITH

Well done, good and faithful servant!
You have been faithful with a few things;
I will put you in charge of many things.

MATTHEW 25:21 NIV

Do well the little things now and then great things
will come to you by and by asking to be done.

PERSIAN PROVERB

God's Path

Listen...and be wise, and keep your
heart on the right path.

PROVERBS 23:19 NIV

Make no little plans; they have no magic
to stir men's blood and probably themselves
will not be realized. Make big plans; aim high
in hope and work, remembering that a noble,
logical diagram once recorded will not die.

DANIEL H. BURNHAM

In his heart a man plans his course,
but the LORD determines his steps.

PROVERBS 16:9 NIV

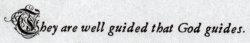

They are well guided that God guides.

SCOTTISH PROVERB

God goes to those who come to Him.

RUSSIAN PROVERB

God's wisdom is always available to help
us choose from alternatives we face, and help
us to follow His eternal plan for us.

GLORIA GAITHER

The very steps we take come from GOD;
otherwise how would we know where we're going?

PROVERBS 20:24 MSG

Whoever walks toward God one step,
God runs toward him two.

JEWISH PROVERB

Your word is a lamp to my feet and a light for my path.

PSALM 119:105 NIV

God's Word acts as a light for our paths.
It can help scare off unwanted thoughts
in our minds and protect us from the enemy.

GARY SMALLEY AND JOHN TRENT

Practical Victory

We are conscious of our own weakness and of the strength of evil; but not of the third force, stronger than either ourselves or the power of evil, which is at our disposal if we will draw upon it. What is needed is a deliberate and whole-hearted realization that we are *in Christ*, and Christ is *in us* by His Spirit. We need an unconditional surrender of faith to Him; a practice, which grows more natural by exercise, of remembering and deliberately drawing by faith upon His strength in the moments of temptation and not merely upon our own resources.... So we too may form, like St. Paul, the habit of victory.

CHARLES GORE

You have given me your shield of victory.
Your right hand supports me.

PSALM 18:35 NLT

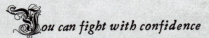 *ou can fight with confidence
where you are sure of victory.
With Christ and for Christ victory is certain.*

BERNARD OF CLAIRVAUX

Thanks be to God, who gives us the victory
through our Lord Jesus Christ.

1 CORINTHIANS 15:57 NASB

Victory becomes, to some degree, a state of mind.
Knowing ourselves superior to the anxieties, troubles,
and worries which obsess us, we are superior to them.

BASIL KING

Every Need

God wants nothing from us except our needs,
and these furnish Him with room to display
His bounty when He supplies them freely....
Not what I have, but what I do not have, is the first
point of contact between my soul and God.

CHARLES H. SPURGEON

Do not worry about anything, but pray and ask God
for everything you need, always giving thanks. And
God's peace, which is so great we cannot understand
it, will keep your hearts and minds in Christ Jesus.

PHILIPPIANS 4:6–7 NCV

*Jesus Christ has brought every need,
every joy, every gratitude, every hope of ours
before God. He accompanies us and brings
us into the presence of God.*

DIETRICH BONHOEFFER

He himself gives life and breath to everything,
and he satisfies every need.

ACTS 17:25 NLT

The "air" which our souls need also envelops
all of us at all times and on all sides.
God is round about us...on every hand,
with many-sided and all-sufficient grace.

OLE HALLESBY

And my God will supply all your needs according
to His riches in glory in Christ Jesus.

PHILIPPIANS 4:19 NASB

Stand still...and refuse to retreat.
Look at it as God looks at it and draw upon
His power to hold up under the blast.

CHARLES SWINDOLL

Contentment

Contentment is not the fulfillment of what you want,
but the realization of how much you already have.

Godliness with contentment is great gain.
For we brought nothing into the world,
and we can take nothing out of it. But if we have
food and clothing, we will be content with that.

1 TIMOTHY 6:6–8 NIV

If we are cheerful and contented, all nature smiles...
the flowers are more fragrant, the birds sing
more sweetly, and the sun, moon, and stars all appear
more beautiful, and seem to rejoice with us.

ORISON SWETT MARDEN

God wants us to be present where we are.
He invites us to see and to hear what is around us and,
through it all, to discern the footprints of the Holy.

RICHARD J. FOSTER

I have learned to be content in whatever circumstances I am. I know how to get along with humble means, and I also know how to live in prosperity; in any and every circumstance I have learned the secret of being filled and going hungry, both of having abundance and suffering need. I can do all things through Him who strengthens me.

PHILIPPIANS 4:11–13 NASB

Know by the light of faith that God is present, and be content with directing all your actions toward Him.

BROTHER LAWRENCE

What Lies Within

It is not in the pursuit of happiness that we find
fulfillment, it is in the happiness of pursuit.

DENIS WAITLEY

He who pursues righteousness and love finds life,
prosperity and honor.

PROVERBS 21:21 NIV

A span of life is nothing. But the man or woman who
lives that span, they are something. They can fill that
tiny span with meaning, so its quality is immeasurable,
though its quantity may be insignificant.

CHAIM POTOK

And I pray that you...will have the power to
understand the greatness of Christ's love—how wide
and how long and how high and how deep that love
is.... Then you can be filled with the fullness of God.

EPHESIANS 3:18–19 NCV

What lies behind us and what lies before us are
tiny matters compared to what lies within us.

RALPH WALDO EMERSON

*You're blessed when you're content with
just who you are—no more, no less.
That's the moment you find yourselves proud
owners of everything that can't be bought.*

MATTHEW 5:5 MSG

Vision looks inwards and becomes duty.
Vision looks outwards and becomes aspiration.
Vision looks upwards and becomes faith.

STEPHEN SAMUEL WISE

I will give them singleness of heart and put a new spirit
within them. I will take away their stony, stubborn
heart and give them a tender, responsive heart.

EZEKIEL 11:19 NLT

Good Courage

Should we feel at times disheartened and
discouraged, a simple movement of heart toward
God will renew our powers. Whatever He may
demand of us, He will give us at the moment
the strength and courage that we need.

FRANÇOIS FÉNELON

Be strong and courageous!
Do not be afraid or discouraged.
For the LORD your God is with you wherever you go.

JOSHUA 1:9 NLT

We walk without fear, full of hope
and courage and strength to do His will, waiting
for the endless good which He is always giving
as fast as He can get us able to take it in.

GEORGE MACDONALD

Be of good courage, all is before you,
and time passed in the difficult is never lost....
What is required of us is that we live the difficult
and learn to deal with it. In the difficult are the
friendly forces, the hands that work on us.

RAINER MARIA RILKE

For You, LORD,
have made me glad through Your work;
I will triumph in the works of Your hands.

PSALM 92:4–5 NKJV

With each new experience of letting God
be in control, we gain courage and reinforcement
for daring to do it again and again.

GLORIA GAITHER

In His Likeness

In the very beginning it was God who formed
us by His Word. He made us in His own image.
God was spirit and He gave us a spirit so that He could
come into us and mingle His own life with our life.

MADAME JEANNE GUYON

The God of the universe—the One who created
everything and holds it all in His hand—created
each of us in His image, to bear His likeness,
His imprint. It is only when Christ dwells within
our hearts, radiating the pure light of His love
through our humanity, that we discover who
we are and what we were intended to be.

WENDY MOORE

Let him take hold of my strength,
that he may make peace with me.

ISAIAH 27:5 KJV

For in Him all the fullness of Deity dwells in bodily
form, and in Him you have been made complete.

COLOSSIANS 2:9–10 NASB

God looks at the world through the eyes of love.
If we, therefore, as human beings made in the image
of God also want to see reality rationally,
that is, as it truly is, then we, too,
must learn to look at what we see with love.

ROBERTA BONDI

By Integrity

It's the life behind the words that makes
the testimony effective.

In my integrity you uphold me and set me
in your presence forever. Praise be to the LORD,
the God of Israel, from everlasting to everlasting.

PSALM 41:12–13 NIV

God is first of all concerned with what you are.
What you do is the result of what you are.

BILLY GRAHAM

There may be no trumpet sound or loud applause
when we make a right decision, just a calm sense
of resolution and peace.

GLORIA GAITHER

*I know, my God, that you examine our hearts
and rejoice when you find integrity there.*

1 CHRONICLES 29:17 NLT

God has given us two ways to communicate—
with words and with actions.
We need both to do the job right.

JANETTE OKE

For only the godly will live in the land,
and those with integrity will remain in it.

PROVERBS 2:21 NLT

Beautiful thoughts hardly bring us to God
until they are acted upon. No one can
have a true idea of right until he does it.

WILLIAM R. INGE

Stick to It

Success is failure turned inside out,
The silver tint of the clouds of doubt,
And you never can tell how close you are,
It may be near when it seems so far.
So stick to the fight when you're hardest hit,
It's when things seem worst
That you must not quit.

You, O God, are both tender and kind, not easily
angered, immense in love, and you never, never quit.

PSALM 86:15 MSG

*The Promised Land belongs to the person
who takes the risks, whose face is marred
by dust and sweat, who strives valiantly
while daring everything.*

TONY CAMPOLO

Anyone who meets a testing challenge head-on
and manages to stick it out is mighty fortunate.
For such persons loyally in love with God,
the reward is life and more life.

JAMES 1:12 MSG

If we permit society to define success and
fulfillment for us, we become sheep with a
shepherd whose definition is 180 degrees from
God's. The Christian must not possess an inner
motivation based on image, status, possessions,
or accomplishments, but rather on being
faithful to what God has asked him to do.

JEAN FLEMING

The LORD rewards every man for his
righteousness and faithfulness.

1 SAMUEL 26:23 NIV

The Goodness of God

The goodness of God is infinitely more wonderful
than we will ever be able to comprehend.

A. W. TOZER

I am still confident of this: I will see the goodness of
the LORD in the land of the living. Wait for the LORD;
be strong and take heart and wait for the LORD.

PSALM 27:13–14 NIV

All that is good, all that is true, all that is beautiful,
all that is beneficent, be it great or small, be it perfect
or fragmentary, natural as well as supernatural,
moral as well as material, comes from God.

JOHN HENRY NEWMAN

How great is your goodness, which you have stored
up for those who fear you, which you bestow in the
sight of men on those who take refuge in you.

PSALM 31:19 NIV

We walk without fear, full of hope and courage
and strength to do His will, waiting for the endless
good which He is always giving as fast as He can
get us able to take it in.

GEORGE MACDONALD

Open your mouth and taste, open your eyes
and see—how good GOD is. Blessed are you who
run to him. Worship God if you want the best;
worship opens doors to all his goodness.

PSALM 34:8–9 MSG

New Every Morning

O LORD, be gracious to us; we long for you.
Be our strength every morning,
our salvation in time of distress.

ISAIAH 33:2 NIV

Ah, Hope! what would life be, stripped
of your encouraging smiles, that teach us to
look behind the dark clouds of today,
for the golden beams that are to gild the morrow.

SUSANNA MOODIE

Hold on, my child! Joy comes in the morning!
Weeping only lasts for the night....
The darkest hour means dawn is just in sight!

GLORIA GAITHER

Weeping may remain for a night,
but rejoicing comes in the morning.

PSALM 30:5 NIV

When morning gilds the skies,
My heart awaking cries:
May Jesus Christ be praised!

JOSEPH BARNBY

Then your light will break forth like the dawn,
and your healing will quickly appear; then your
righteousness will go before you, and the glory of the
LORD will be your rear guard.

ISAIAH 58:8 NIV

That is God's call to us—simply to be people who are
content to live close to Him and to renew the kind of
life in which the closeness is felt and experienced.

THOMAS MERTON

The faithful love of the LORD never ends!
His mercies never cease.
Great is his faithfulness; his mercies begin
afresh each morning.

LAMENTATIONS 3:22–23 NLT

Learn to Lead

The best way to lead is by a good example.

Among you it will be different. Whoever wants
to be a leader among you must be your servant.

MARK 10:43 NLT

*Leaders learn by leading, and they learn best
by leading in the face of obstacles. As weather
shapes mountains, problems shape leaders.*

WARREN G. BENNIS

Consider it pure joy...whenever you face trials
of many kinds, because you know that the testing
of your faith develops perseverance. Perseverance must
finish its work so that you may be mature
and complete, not lacking anything.

JAMES 1:2–4 NIV

The first responsibility of a leader is to define reality.
The last is to say thank you.
In between, the leader is a servant.

MAX DE PREE

Remember those who led you, who spoke the word
of God to you; and considering the result of their
conduct, imitate their faith.

HEBREWS 13:7 NASB

If leaders are filled with high ambition and if they
pursue their aims with audacity and strength of will,
they will reach them in spite of all obstacles.

CARL VON CLAUSEWITZ

Pursue a righteous life—a life of wonder,
faith, love, steadiness, courtesy. Run hard and fast
in the faith. Seize the eternal life, the life you
were called to, the life you so fervently embraced
in the presence of so many witnesses.

1 TIMOTHY 6:11–12 MSG

Think on These Things

Brothers...think about the things that are
good and worthy of praise. Think about
the things that are true and honorable and right
and pure and beautiful and respected.

PHILIPPIANS 4:8 NCV

Only to sit and think of God,
Oh what a joy it is!
To think the thought,
To breathe the Name:
Earth has no higher bliss.

FREDERICK W. FABER

Oh, how I love your instructions! I think about
them all day long.... How sweet your words
taste to me; they are sweeter than honey.

PSALM 119:97, 103 NLT

The happiness of your life depends upon
the character of your thoughts.

Guard Clear Thinking and Common Sense with
your life; don't for a minute lose sight of them.
They'll keep your soul alive and well,
they'll keep you fit and attractive.

PROVERBS 3:21–22 MSG

When I think upon my God, my heart is so full
of joy that the notes dance and leap from my pen.

FRANZ JOSEF HAYDN

You have made known to me the ways of life;
You will make me full of joy in Your presence.

ACTS 2:28 NKJV

Though we cannot be always thinking of God,
we may be always employed in His service.
There must be intervals of our communion
with Him, but there must be no intermission
of our attachment to Him.

HANNAH MORE

Experience Hope

You are not here merely to make a living. You are here in order to enable the world to live more amply, with greater vision, with a finer spirit of hope and achievement. You are here to enrich the world, and you impoverish yourself if you forget the errand.

WOODROW WILSON

I pray for you constantly, asking God, the glorious Father of our Lord Jesus Christ, to give you spiritual wisdom and insight so that you might grow in your knowledge of God. I pray that your hearts will be flooded with light so that you can understand the confident hope he has given to those he called—his holy people who are his rich and glorious inheritance. I also pray that you will understand the incredible greatness of God's power for us who believe him.

EPHESIANS 1:16–19 NLT

I asked for strength that I might achieve;
I was made weak that I might learn humbly to obey.
I asked for health that I might do greater things;
I was given infirmity that I might do better things.
I asked for riches that I might be wise.
I asked for power that I might feel the need of God.
I asked for all things that I might enjoy all things.
I got nothing that I asked for,
But everything that I had hoped for.
Almost despite myself my unspoken prayers
were answered;
I am, among all men, most richly blessed.

UNKNOWN CONFEDERATE SOLDIER

May the God of hope fill you with all joy and peace as you trust in him, so that you may overflow with hope by the power of the Holy Spirit.

ROMANS 15:13 NIV

Faith Adventure

Faith sees the invisible, believes the incredible,
and receives the impossible.

In this you greatly rejoice, though now for a little
while you may have had to suffer grief in all kinds
of trials. These have come so that your faith—
of greater worth than gold, which perishes even though
refined by fire—may be proved genuine and may
result in praise, glory and honor when Jesus Christ
is revealed. Though you have not seen him, you love
him; and even though you do not see him now,
you believe in him and are filled with an inexpressible
and glorious joy, for you are receiving the goal
of your faith, the salvation of your souls.

1 PETER 1:6–9 NIV

Faith means you want God and want to want nothing
else.... In faith there is movement and development.
Each day something is new.

BRENNAN MANNING

There will always be the unknown.
There will always be the unprovable. But faith
confronts those frontiers with a thrilling leap.
Then life becomes vibrant with adventure!

ROBERT SCHULLER

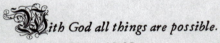ith God all things are possible.

MARK 10:27 KJV

God wants us to approach life, full of expectancy
that God is going to be at work in every situation
as we grow in our faith in Him.

COLIN URQUHART

Faith is not a sense, not sight, not reason,
but a taking God at His Word.

FAITH EVANS

A Worthwhile Life

I wish you humor and a twinkle in the eye. I wish
you glory and the strength to bear its burdens. I wish
you sunshine on your path and storms to season your
journey. I wish you peace—in the world in which
you live and in the smallest corner of the heart where
truth is kept. I wish you faith—to help define your
living and your life. More I cannot wish you—
except perhaps love—to make all the rest worthwhile.

ROBERT A. WARD

Everything that goes into a life of pleasing God has
been miraculously given to us by getting to know,
personally and intimately, the One who invited us to
God. The best invitation we ever received! We were
also given absolutely terrific promises to pass on to you.

2 PETER 1:3 MSG

Real joy comes not from ease or riches or from the praise of people, but from doing something worthwhile.

WILFRED GRENWELL

I consider everything a loss compared to the surpassing greatness of knowing Christ Jesus my Lord.

PHILIPPIANS 3:8 NIV

What makes life worthwhile is having a big enough objective, something which catches our imagination and lays hold of our allegiance.... What higher, more exalted, and more compelling goal can there be than to know God?

J. I. PACKER

Live Well

What constitutes success? He has achieved success
who has lived well; laughed often and loved much;
who has gained the respect of intelligent men and
the love of little children; who has filled his niche
and accomplished his task; who has left the world
better than he found it, whether by an improved
poppy, a perfect poem or a rescued soul; who has
never lacked appreciation of earth's beauty, or failed
to express it; who has always looked for the best in
others and given the best he had; whose life was an
inspiration; whose memory a benediction.

BESSIE ANDERSON STANLEY

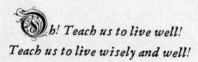

Oh! Teach us to live well!
Teach us to live wisely and well!

PSALM 90:12 MSG

Success is neither fame, wealth nor power;
rather it is seeking, knowing, loving and obeying
God. If you seek, you will know; if you know,
you will love; if you love, you will obey.

CHARLES MALIK

Oh, the joys of those who do not follow the
advice of the wicked, or...join in with mockers.
But they delight in the law of the LORD,
meditating on it day and night. They are like
trees planted along the riverbank, bearing fruit
each season.... They prosper in all they do.

PSALM 1:1–3 NLT

When a man feels throbbing within him the
power to do what he undertakes as well as it can
possibly be done, this is happiness, this is success.

ORISON SWETT MARDEN

A Wonderful Future

Those who build the future are those who know
that greater things are yet to come, and that they
themselves will help bring them about.

MELVIN J. EVANS

Look at those who are honest and good, for a
wonderful future awaits those who love peace.

PSALM 37:37 NLT

Learn from the past, work for the present,
and plan for the future.

JANETTE OKE

Guide me in your truth and teach me...my hope
is in you all day long. Remember, O LORD, your great
mercy and love, for they are from of old.

PSALM 25:5–6 NIV

You can never change the past. But by the grace
of God, you can win the future. So remember those
things which will help you forward, but forget those
things which will only hold you back.

RICHARD C. WOODSOME

And through your faith, God is protecting you
by his power until you receive this salvation....
So be truly glad. There is wonderful joy ahead.

1 PETER 1:5–6 NLT

Each day can be the beginning of a wonderful future.

I have it all planned out—plans to take care of you,
not abandon you,
plans to give you the future you hope for.

JEREMIAH 29:11 MSG

Dreams Fulfilled

Lift up your eyes. Your heavenly Father waits
to bless you—in inconceivable ways to make
your life what you never dreamed it could be.

ANNE ORTLUND

I came so they can have real and eternal life,
more and better life than they ever dreamed of.

JOHN 10:10 MSG

God created us with an overwhelming desire to soar....
He designed us to be tremendously productive
and "to mount up with wings like eagles," realistically
dreaming of what He can do with our potential.

CAROL KENT

Those who hope in the LORD
will renew their strength.
They will soar on wings like eagles;
they will run and not grow weary,
they will walk and not be faint.

ISAIAH 40:31 NIV

God is not an elusive dream or a phantom
to chase, but a divine person to know.
He does not avoid us,
but seeks us. When we seek Him,
the contact is instantaneous.

NEVA COYLE

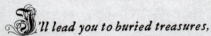 *I'll lead you to buried treasures,*
secret caches of valuables —
Confirmations that it is, in fact, I, God...
who calls you by your name.

ISAIAH 45:3 MSG

To dream anything that you want to dream.
That is the beauty of the human mind.
To do anything that you want to do. That is the
strength of the human will. To trust yourself to test
your limits. That is the courage to succeed.

BERNARD EDMONDS

Friendship with God

Friendship with God is a two-way street.... Jesus said
that He tells His friends all that His Father has
told Him; close friends communicate thoroughly
and make a transfer of heart and thought. How
awesome is our opportunity to be friends with God,
the almighty Creator of all!

BEVERLY LAHAYE

Become friends with God;
he's already a friend with you.

2 CORINTHIANS 5:20 MSG

God's friendship is the unexpected joy we find
when we reach His outstretched hand.

JANET L. SMITH

Steep yourself in God-reality, God-initiative,
God-provisions.... You're my dearest friends!
The Father wants to give you the very kingdom itself.

LUKE 12:31–32 MSG

*I have called you friends,
for all things that I have heard from My Father
I have made known to you.*

JOHN 15:15 NASB

We can look to God as our Father. We can have a
personal sense of His love for us and His interest in us,
for He is concerned about us as a father is concerned
for his children.... Incredible as it may seem, God wants
our companionship. He wants to have us close to Him.
He wants to be a father to us, to shield us, to protect us,
to counsel us, and to guide us in our way through life.

BILLY GRAHAM

United

Other men are lenses through
which we read our own minds.

RALPH WALDO EMERSON

Keep on loving each other as brothers.

HEBREWS 13:1 NIV

A friend is a gift you give yourself.

ROBERT LOUIS STEVENSON

It is absolutely clear that God has called you to a free
life. Just make sure that you don't use this freedom as
an excuse to do whatever you want to do and destroy
your freedom. Rather, use your freedom to serve one
another in love; that's how freedom grows.

GALATIANS 5:13 MSG

*God can show Himself as He really is only
to real men. And that means not simply to men
who are individually good, but to men
who are united together in a body, loving
one another, showing him to one another.
For that is what God meant humanity to be like;
like players in one band, or organs in one body.*

C. S. LEWIS

Let me be united with all who fear you,
with those who know your laws.

PSALM 119:79 NLT

The firmest friendships have been formed
in mutual adversity; as iron is most strongly
united by the fiercest flame.

CHARLES CALEB COLTON

In His Hand

The mystery of life is that the Lord of life cannot
be known except in and through the act of living.
Without the concrete and specific involvements of
daily life we cannot come to know the loving presence
of Him who holds us in the palm of His hand....
Therefore, we are called each day to present
to our Lord the whole of our lives.

HENRI J. M. NOUWEN

*Behold, I have inscribed you
on the palms of My hands.*

ISAIAH 49:16 NASB

I'm a little pencil in the hands of a loving
God who is writing a love letter to the world.

MOTHER TERESA

God promises to keep us in the palm of His hand, with
or without our awareness. God has already made a space
for us, even if we have not made a space for God.

DAVID AND BARBARA SORENSEN

Do not fear, for I am with you; do not be dismayed,
for I am your God. I will strengthen you and help you;
I will uphold you with my righteous right hand.

ISAIAH 41:10 NIV

The God who holds the whole world in His hands
wraps Himself in the splendor of the sun's light
and walks among the clouds.

That Hand which bears all nature up
Shall guard His children well.

WILLIAM COWPER

Good Gifts

Gratitude consists in a watchful, minute attention
to the particulars of our state, and to the multitude of
God's gifts, taken one by one. It fills us with
a consciousness that God loves and cares for us,
even to the least event and smallest need of life.

HENRY EDWARD MANNING

All God's gifts are right in front of you
as you wait expectantly for our Master Jesus....
And not only that, but God himself is right
alongside to keep you steady and on track.

1 CORINTHIANS 1:7–8 MSG

To be grateful is to recognize the Love of God in
everything He has given us—and He has given us
everything. Every breath we draw is a gift of His love,
every moment of existence is a gift of grace.

THOMAS MERTON

For who do you know that really knows you, knows your heart? And even if they did, is there anything they would discover in you that you could take credit for? Isn't everything you have and everything you are sheer gifts from God?

1 CORINTHIANS 4:7 MSG

As God loves a cheerful giver,
so He also loves a cheerful taker,
who takes hold on His gifts with a glad heart.

JOHN DONNE

Let them give thanks to the LORD
for his unfailing love...for he satisfies the thirsty
and fills the hungry with good things.

PSALM 107:8–9 NIV

Live Fully

The greatest honor we can give God is to live
gladly because of the knowledge of His love.

JULIAN OF NORWICH

Love GOD, your God. Walk in his ways. Keep his
commandments, regulations, and rules so that you will
live, really live, live exuberantly, blessed by GOD.

DEUTERONOMY 30:16 MSG

It is not a difficult matter to learn what it means
to delight ourselves in the Lord. It is to live so
as to please Him, to honor everything we find
in His Word, to do everything the way He would
like to have it done, and for Him.

S. MAXWELL CODER

Delight yourself also in the LORD, and He shall give you the desires of your heart. Commit your way to the LORD, trust also in Him, and He shall bring it to pass.

PSALM 37:4–5 NKJV

By living fully, recognizing that all we do is by His [God's] power, we honor Him; He in turn blesses us.

BECKY LAIRD

We all live off his generous bounty, gift after gift after gift.

JOHN 1:16 MSG

I consider beyond all wealth, honor, or even health, is the attachment due to noble souls; because to become one with the good, generous, and true, is to be, in a manner, good, generous, and true yourself.

THOMAS ARNOLD

Joy and Strength

Our hearts were made for joy. Our hearts were made
to enjoy the One who created them. Too deeply
planted to be much affected by the ups and downs
of life, this joy is a knowing and a being known by
our Creator. He sets our hearts alight with radiant joy.

Surely you have granted him eternal blessings
and made him glad with the joy of your presence.

PSALM 21:6 NIV

If one is joyful, it means that one is faithfully living
for God, and that nothing else counts; and if one
gives joy to others one is doing God's work.
With joy without and joy within, all is well.

JANET ERSKINE STUART

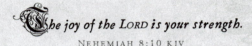

The joy of the LORD is your strength.

NEHEMIAH 8:10 KJV

Live for today but hold your hands open to tomorrow.
Anticipate the future and its changes with joy.
There is a seed of God's love in every event,
every circumstance, every unpleasant situation
in which you may find yourself.

BARBARA JOHNSON

Satisfy us in the morning with your unfailing love,
that we may sing for joy and be glad all our days.

PSALM 90:14 NIV

Joy is the holy fire that keeps our purpose
warm and our intelligence aglow.

HELEN KELLER

Heavenly Roses

Honor women! They entwine and weave
heavenly roses in our earthly life.

JOHANN SCHILLER

Charm is deceptive, and beauty is fleeting;
but a woman who fears the LORD is to be praised.

PROVERBS 31:30 NIV

Let men beware of causing women to weep;
God counts their tears.

HEBREW PROVERB

A good woman is hard to find, and worth far more
than diamonds. Her husband trusts her without reserve,
and never has reason to regret it. Never spiteful,
she treats him generously all her life long.

PROVERBS 31:10–12 MSG

Men must understand that women tend to care more
than they about the home and everything in it.

JAMES DOBSON

Nothing is won by force. I choose to be gentle.
If I raise my voice may it be only in praise.
If I clench my fist, may it be only in prayer.
If I make a demand, may it be only of myself.

MAX LUCADO

Then the LORD God made a woman from
the rib, and he brought her to the man.
"At last!" the man exclaimed.

GENESIS 2:22–23 NLT

Among the Lord's people, women are not independent
of men, and men are not independent of women.

1 CORINTHIANS 11:11 NLT

*In the heart of every man is a desperate
desire for a battle to fight, an adventure to live,
and a beauty to rescue.*

JOHN ELDREDGE

Different Gifts

Everyone has a unique role to fill in the world
and is important in some respect. Everyone,
including and perhaps especially you, is indispensable.

NATHANIEL HAWTHORNE

*Just as each of us has one body with
many members, and these members do not
all have the same function, so in Christ
we who are many form one body, and each
member belongs to all the others. We have
different gifts, according to the grace given us.*

ROMANS 12:4–6 NIV

What we are is God's gift to us.
What we become is our gift to God.

ELEANOR POWELL

For the LORD God is our sun and our shield.
He gives us grace and glory. The LORD will withhold
no good thing from those who do what is right.

PSALM 84:11 NLT

I pray that from His glorious, unlimited resources
He will empower you with inner strength through
His Spirit. Then Christ will make his home in your
hearts as you trust in Him. Your roots will grow
down into God's love and keep you strong.

EPHESIANS 3:16–17 NLT

God has a wonderful plan
for each person He has chosen.

LOUISE B. WYLY

A Reputation

Reputation is what folks think you are. Personality is what you seem to be. Character is what you really are.

ALFRED ARMAND MONTAPERT

If I take care of my character,
my reputation will take care of itself.

DWIGHT L. MOODY

Don't lose a minute in building on what
you've been given, complementing your basic
faith with good character, spiritual understanding,
alert discipline, passionate patience, reverent wonder,
warm friendliness, and generous love, each dimension
fitting into and developing the others.

2 PETER 1:5–7 MSG

Regard your good name as the richest jewel you can possibly be possessed of—for credit is like fire; when once you have kindled it you may easily preserve it, but if you extinguish it, you will find it an arduous task to rekindle it again. The way to gain a good reputation is to endeavor to be what you desire to appear.

SOCRATES

A wise person gets known for insight;
gracious words add to one's reputation.

PROVERBS 16:21 MSG

Character is like a tree and reputation like its shadow. The shadow is what we think of it; the tree is the real thing.

ABRAHAM LINCOLN

Happy and Thankful

It is not how much we have, but how
much we enjoy, that makes happiness.

CHARLES H. SPURGEON

In him our hearts rejoice,
for we trust in his holy name.
May your unfailing love rest upon us, O LORD,
even as we put our hope in you.

PSALM 33:21–22 NIV

We find greatest joy, not in getting, but in expressing
what we are. Men do not really live for honors
or for pay; their gladness is not the taking and holding,
but in the doing, the striving, the building, the living....
The happy man is he who lives the life of love,
not for the honors it may bring, but for the life itself.

R. J. BAUGHAN

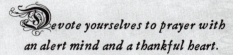*evote yourselves to prayer with an alert mind and a thankful heart.*

COLOSSIANS 4:2 NLT

Our inner happiness depends not on what we experience but on the degree of our gratitude to God, whatever the experience.

ALBERT SCHWEITZER

I will bless the LORD at all times:
his praise shall continually be in my mouth.

PSALM 34:1 KJV

Maybe we could spend a moment at the end of each day and decide to remember that day—whatever may have happened—as a day to be grateful for. In so doing we increase our heart's capacity to choose joy.

HENRI J. M. NOUWEN

Hard Work

Work is the natural exercise and function of man....
Work is not primarily a thing one does to live, but
the thing one lives to do. It is, or should be, the full
expression of the worker's faculties, the thing in which
he finds spiritual, mental and bodily satisfaction, and the
medium in which he offers himself to God.

DOROTHY L. SAYERS

Far and away the best prize that life offers
is the chance to work hard at work worth doing.

THEODORE ROOSEVELT

He performs wonders that cannot be fathomed,
miracles that cannot be counted.

JOB 5:9 NIV

Miracles come after a lot of hard work.

SUE BENDER

It is not the work we do that is so important. It's the
people we work with. It's the work God does in our
lives through them. And it's the work He does in their
lives through us. That is what's sacred. Slowing down
and stopping is our way of acknowledging it.

KEN GIRE

*Whatever you do, work at it with all your
heart, as working for the Lord, not for men,
since you know that you will receive an inheritance
from the Lord as a reward.
It is the Lord Christ you are serving.*

COLOSSIANS 3:23–24 NIV

I Will Sustain You

We know certainly that our God calls
us to a holy life. We know that He gives
us every grace, every abundant grace;
and though we are so weak of ourselves,
this grace is able to carry us through
every obstacle and difficulty.

ELIZABETH ANN SETON

Take my yoke upon you. Let me teach you,
because I am humble and gentle at heart,
and you will find rest for your souls.

MATTHEW 11:29 NLT

They travel lightly whom God's grace carries.

THOMAS à KEMPIS

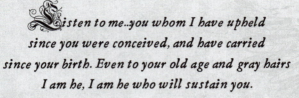

Listen to me..you whom I have upheld
since you were conceived, and have carried
since your birth. Even to your old age and gray hairs
I am he, I am he who will sustain you.

ISAIAH 46:3–4 NIV

I have learned that faith means trusting
in advance what will only make sense in reverse.

PHILIP YANCEY

I could see only one set of footprints,
So I said to the Lord, "You promised me,
Lord, that if I followed You,
You would walk with me always...."
The Lord replied,
"The times when you have seen only
one set of footprints
Is when I carried you."

ELLA H. SCHARRING-HAUSEN

An Invitation

If you have ever:

questioned if this is all there is to life...

wondered what happens when you die...

felt a longing for purpose or significance...

wrestled with resurfacing anger...

struggled to forgive someone...

known there is a "higher power" but couldn't define it...

sensed you have a role to play in the world...

experienced success and still felt empty afterward...

then consider Jesus.

A great teacher from two millennia ago, Jesus of Nazareth, the Son of God, freely chose to show our Maker's everlasting love for us by offering to take all of our flaws, darkness, death, and mistakes into His very body (1 Peter 2:24). The result was His death on a cross. But the story doesn't end there. God raised Him from the dead and invites us to believe this truth in our hearts and follow Jesus into eternal life.

If you confess with your mouth that Jesus is Lord and believe in your heart that God raised him from the dead, you will be saved. —ROMANS 10:9 NLT